C000131860

)UP

Bible Genres

HEARING WHAT THE BIBLE REALLY SAYS

CWR

Andy Peck

Copyright © CWR 2013

Published 2013 by CWR, Waverley Abbey House, Waverley Lane, Farnham, Surrey GU9 8EP, UK. CWR is a Registered Charity – Number 294387 and a Limited Company registered in England – Registration Number 1990308.

The right of Andy Peck to be identified as the author of this work has been asserted by him in accordance with the Copyright, Designs and Patents Act 1988, sections 77 and 78.

All rights reserved. No part of this publication may be reproduced, stored in a retrieval system, or transmitted, in any form or by any means, electronic, mechanical, photocopying, recording or otherwise, without the prior permission in writing of CWR.

See back of book for list of National Distributors.

Unless otherwise indicated, all Scripture references are from the Holy Bible: New International Version (NIV), Copyright © 1979, 1984, 2011 by Biblica (formerly International Bible Society). Used by permission of Hodder & Stoughton Publishers, an Hachette UK company. All rights reserved. 'NIV' is a registered trademark of Biblica (formerly International Bible Society). UK trademark number 1448790.

Concept development, editing, design and production by CWR.

Cover image: Fotosearch

Printed in the UK by Page Brothers

ISBN: 978-1-85345-987-0

Contents

Introduction

You have probably heard preachers use the phrase 'the Bible says' before going on to quote a Bible text. Using the phrase 'the Bible says' when quoting a Bible verse is partly accurate, but only partly. Potentially, speakers are falling for a basic fallacy of reading and interpreting the Bible which can cause a great deal of anguish and pain. Why do I say this? 'Bible' is a word that literally means 'library of books'. It is, of course, a special library; a God-breathed library with a unity and message that makes it unlike any other book collection. In one sense, there is a sole author; God Himself. But the danger of 'the Bible says' language is that you approach the Bible assuming that all texts are the same, which they plainly are not. You cannot assert 'the Bible says' without making sure you read and interpret the quoted text as it was originally given.

For example, Ecclesiastes 8:15 says: 'So I commend the enjoyment of life, because there is nothing better for a person under the sun than to eat and drink and be glad.' Is that really true? Doesn't Scripture itself suggest there is more to life than eating and drinking? Deuteronomy 22:11 says: 'Do not wear clothes of wool and linen woven together' which might suggest that many of us need to change our wardrobe! Or how about Psalm 137:9 that suggests, 'Happy is the one who seizes your infants and dashes them against the rocks'?

Claiming that 'the Bible says', preachers have justified slavery, wife beating, apartheid, dictatorial leadership, pacifism, military action, poverty and prosperity. Many have been led astray, confused and disheartened by a particular view, or merely bemused that Christians disagree. It all suggests that we take our spiritual life into our hands more than we imagine when we wade into reading the Bible!

Part of the answer to these issues is to realise that God uses the personalities of many authors writing in particular styles to convey His truth. The 'library' has many types of genre and the books in the library sometimes employ more than one style within a book. If we grasp the genre we will be better able to understand what the writer of the text intended. In comparing this with other writers, we can then develop a perspective on the main and plain things of Scripture without getting sidetracked. This won't solve all the problems, but it will lessen our propensity to make foolish and potentially painful errors in interpretation.

Through this seven-study *Cover to Cover* format, we will explore the following genres: law, narrative, psalm, prophecy, gospel, epistle and apocalyptic writing, enabling us to consider most of the major genre types. It is not exhaustive – a case could be made for studying 'wisdom literature', as presented in Proverbs, Ecclesiastes, Song of Songs, and some of the Psalms. The psalm category, comprising largely poetry, (which is also used in other parts of Scripture, notably the prophets) is not actually a literary genre as such. However, I chose Psalms in preference to wisdom literature because of its traditional importance to the Christian Church in worship and personal devotions.

Gospel, a category we also investigate, is in many people's minds a form of narrative. But although each Gospel has a clear narrative framework, culminating in a focus on the last week of Jesus' earthly life, most scholars recognise that the gospel genre is unique and worthy of a separate focus. This is not least because many of us think we know the story of Jesus, although we may have little idea why there are four Gospels and what each writer brings to the party. We do not have space to examine parables, a literary genre within the Gospels and other parts of Scripture that has led to much scholarly debate.

As we have noted, genre studies inevitably raise key issues regarding the reading of Scriptural text and it may be worth noting one that will crop up during these studies. Our task when we read the Bible is to discern what its authors and editors intended to say to the original hearers and readers before applying it to our own situations. We will often need the help of Bible scholars and teachers if we are to understand how and why they wrote as they did. In the case of Old Testament texts, we may discover that God has a further intention beyond that known by the author (2 Pet. 1:20–21) as the Holy Spirit leads New Testament authors to perceive meanings behind texts not immediately apparent to the authors or to us as readers.

We may know from personal experience that God sometimes uses a phrase from His Word to apply to our lives in ways that cannot have been in the mind of the author: He is God and He can do what He likes. But good exegesis and interpretation insist that a text cannot now mean something which it never meant in the context in which it was written (the immediate and the wider context of the whole of Scripture) so a grasp of literary genre will be a major tool in our study kit.

As we consider Bible genres, let's pray for God's help so that when we are moved to say 'the Bible says' we know it really does, and that God is the one speaking.

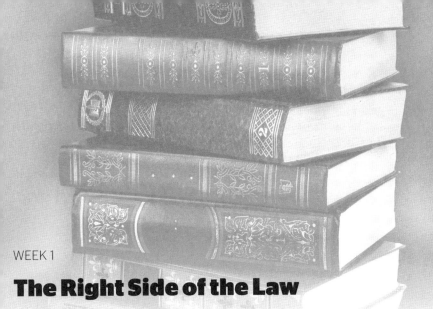

WEEK 1

The Right Side of the Law

Opening Icebreaker

Break into pairs and discuss the oddest rule that you have had to keep, either at home, school or work. Then come back together as a group and vote to establish which rule is the oddest.

Bible Readings

- Exodus 20:1–17
- Deuteronomy 11:1–24
- Leviticus 4:13–26
- Deuteronomy 17:14–20
- Deuteronomy 19:15–21
- Romans 7:1–6

Opening Our Eyes

The word 'law', although used in various ways in Scripture, mostly refers to the laws given to Moses by God when the nation of Israel was formed at Sinai (Exod. 19–20). It is also a title for the first five books of the Bible, known collectively as The Torah, although parts of these books are actually narrative. In the New Testament 'law' is sometimes used as a summary of all God's commands under the old covenant.

Reading the 613 laws that Moses was given at Sinai can be tough because most of them were written for a time and culture dissimilar to our own. We may see the value of the Ten Commandments, but what of laws prohibiting us from wearing clothing with mixed fibres?

As we read and interpret these laws we need to remember the following:

• they were covenant laws
They were given as part of the relationship that God established with those rescued from Egyptian slavery (Exod. 6–14). He invites them to be His people: a model community demonstrating His goodness and love to the world. These laws are God's gracious commands to His people, reflecting His character and wisdom, enabling them to relate to Him as a holy God and enjoy flourishing relationships with each other. The laws may seem restrictive, but they are actually a charter of freedom for former slaves, now living in community.

• ceremonial laws have been superseded
Hundreds of laws regulated the tabernacle (Exod. 25–40), the Levitical/Aaronic priesthood (Exod. 28–30; Lev. 1–9), and the sacrificial system (Lev. 1–7; 16–17; 22:17–30). They remind us of the gravity of sin, that forgiveness

requires a life to be taken and blood to be shed, and they look forward to the day when Jesus will come as God in human flesh, our great High Priest and a sacrifice for sin. They also remind us of the wonder of forgiveness that is enjoyed in Jesus – the book of Hebrews explains that the covenant is obsolete now that we can have this confidence.

• some laws were for that day
Clearly laws regarding mildew in the house, leprosy on the body, and dealing with personal waste belong to that day. However they do remind us that there is no sacred/secular divide, as if God is concerned with worship but not trivial daily matters. They contain principles for living that can benefit us. The apostle Paul notes that the rule about oxen eating grain (Deut. 25:4) has an application for those who preach.

• Christians have a different standing in relation to the law
Christ kept all the demands of the Old Testament Law so by faith in Him we are declared righteous in God's sight. Jesus' death and resurrection brought about a new covenant in which God promises to put His law in our hearts as His Holy Spirit dwells within us.

Paul considers the Law 'good' (Rom. 7:12–13) and 'spiritual' (7:14) explaining that in Christ we come to the Law as those who have confidence in one who kept the Law on our behalf. The Holy Spirit now works, with our co-operation, to make us the kind of people who live the life that God desires. When asked which was the greatest law, Jesus said that all the laws hang on two commands: 'Love the Lord your God with all your heart and with all your soul and with all your mind' and 'Love your neighbour as yourself' (Matt. 22:37–40).

The Spirit of God within the believer helps them do just that.

Discussion Starters

1. How many of the Ten Commandments can you name? Read Exodus 20:1–17 and see how many you recalled.

_____

_____

_____

_____

2. Look at Deuteronomy 11:1–24. What role did laws have for the people of Israel? How might we learn from this approach?

_____

_____

_____

_____

3. Read Leviticus 4:13–26. How do you think Israel would have felt about sin? What is the equivalent practice under the new covenant?

_____

_____

_____

_____

4. Look at Deuteronomy 17:14–20. How did the instructions regarding a king come true for the people of Israel? What do these instructions tell us about the relationship between the law of God and the rulers of God? In what ways might that be abused?

_____

_____

_____

_____

5. Read Deuteronomy 19:15–21. Can you think of illustrations where this practice might have brought about a fair outcome for those unjustly accused?

_____

_____

_____

_____

_____

6. Read Romans 7:1–6. If you had to give a new Christian advice on how they should read the laws of Moses, what would you say?

_____

_____

_____

_____

_____

Personal Application

We now live under a new covenant, although we might actually still function as if we are trying to keep the law of God. You may be secretly wondering whether you measure up to God's demands, or to those of your local church, so it's worth checking your attitude. Remember, you are accepted in Christ who satisfied the requirements of the law completely. From that position of love and acceptance, seek the filling of the Holy Spirit so that you can live the kind of life that reflects a new life in Jesus, with power over sin and a capacity to see His kingdom grow.

Seeing Jesus in the Scriptures

When Jesus said that He had not come to abolish the Law but to fulfil it (Matt. 5:17), His hearers would have understood Him to mean that He came to interpret and apply it correctly. Hence His reminder to the people of Israel that it wasn't enough to be pleased that you hadn't murdered anyone if you had become angry enough to want to commit murder. So Jesus' life in the Gospels demonstrated what God was looking for the Law to achieve, but without the tedious additions that the Jewish teachers had placed alongside it. In the Old Testament 'The Way' was a shorthand description of the Law. Jesus came as '… the way, and the truth and the life' (John 14:6). To people who had sought to keep the Law for generations, this was a lot to get their heads and their hearts around.

Many, though, would come to delight in the glorious truth that we don't need to strive to keep the Law because He has already done so on our behalf.

WEEK 2

God Tells a Good Story

Opening Icebreaker

Using a flip chart, or other means of recording responses, list your favourite stories, either from childhood or more recent years. What makes a good story? Write the answers down.

Bible Readings

- Genesis 12:1–4; 26:3–5,24; 28:14–15
- Exodus 3:1–21
- 1 Samuel 17:1–58
- Acts 1:8; 6:7; 9:31; 12:24; 16:5; 19:20; 28:31

Opening Our Eyes

Everyone loves a good story and the narrative sections are some of the most well-loved in the whole Bible: Moses and the Red Sea, Joshua and the walls of Jericho, David defeating Goliath, Daniel in the lion's den, Nehemiah's re-building of the wall of Jerusalem. Around forty per cent of the Old Testament, a good proportion of the Gospels and most of Acts is written in narrative form. In narrative we sense God's nature and character through His loving interactions with people like us.

But the narratives are more than just interesting stories. We can read them at three levels: the top level can be classified as the 'meta-narrative'. This is the grand, overarching plan of God worked out through human history. It is the story of God's desire to restore His creation when sin entered the world in Genesis 3: through Israel, Jesus, the Church and concluding with God's final restoration of all things in the new heavens and earth, recorded in Revelation.

Beneath this meta-narrative we have the middle level: the breakdown into two testaments – the Old Testament reflecting God's relationship with Israel and the New Testament recounting His sending of Jesus and reflecting His relationship with the Church. The Old Testament narrative covers more than 2,000 years – depending on your date for creation! Much of Genesis through to Deuteronomy and nearly all of Joshua through to Esther is in narrative form. Some of the prophets have narrative portions, eg Isaiah, Jeremiah, Ezekiel, Daniel, Hosea, Jonah and Haggai. Covering around seventy years, the New Testament narrative is much shorter, focusing in the four Gospels on the life, death and resurrection of Jesus, and in Acts on the work of God's Spirit in spreading the news about Jesus throughout the Roman world. Acts finishes in Rome around AD 65. Many of the Epistles are best understood through their place in the Acts narrative.

Finally, the lowest level focuses on the stories of specific individuals within the narrative – the stories that inspire and intrigue us. We need to see this lowest level in the light of the middle narrative, ie where it appears within an unfolding revelation of God in the Old or New Testament, and also how it fits into the meta-narrative. For example, the recounting of Moses and the Red Sea is part of the narrative of God's rescue of the descendants of Abraham from the oppressor, Egypt, but also a symbol of the rescue that God would bring through the death and resurrection of Jesus.

We read the narratives with the imagination and attention that we would give any story, in large enough chunks so that we can appreciate what is being said and what the outcome is. We note any clear literary devices. These include what the narrator of the story emphasises, paying particular attention to dialogue and any repetition of words or ideas.

Recognising these three levels within the biblical text and reading with an eye to the author's aim saves us from treating the narratives like Aesop's fables, as if every narrative has a moral. The narratives are primarily written to give us God's redemptive history, not principles, even though there may be clear lessons for us to draw from the characters of individuals and the outcome of events. Whichever narrative you read, remember that God is always the true hero of any story. It is His purposes and promises that are being furthered.

Discussion Starters

1. Look at the following verses: Genesis 12:1–4; 26:3–5,24; 28:14–15 and Exodus 3:1–21. These verses cover around 500 years of history. How is God's promise expressed in these passages?

    _____
    _____
    _____
    _____
    _____

2. Why is it important to keep the big picture in mind when we read the stories of Abraham, Isaac, Jacob and Moses? What does all this say to you about God?

    _____
    _____
    _____
    _____
    _____

3. Read 1 Samuel 17:1–58. If you were the director of a film which included this scene, what details in the passage would help to bring the scene alive?

    _____
    _____
    _____
    _____
    _____

4. What significance does this scene in 1 Samuel 17 have in the story of David's rise and Saul's demise?

_____

_____

_____

_____

_____

_____

5. In Acts 1:8 we have a summary statement of the whole book: note the summary statements in Acts 6:7; 9:31; 12:24; 16:5; 19:20 and 28:31. What message is Luke conveying through this device?

_____

_____

_____

_____

_____

_____

Personal Application

Stories matter to God, and though your personal story may not have the same universal significance as those of the Bible, it still matters to God. It is useful to reflect on how God has led you, so that you can understand His ways, rejoice in His goodness and perhaps gain clarity for the next stage of your journey. Some people write a daily diary or journal to record their thoughts, prayers and concerns; others take a regular retreat to spend time reflecting on periods of their lives. Maybe you could benefit from taking stock in some way on a regular basis.

Seeing Jesus in the Scriptures

All Bible narrative needs to be seen in the light of the coming of Jesus. Some commentators make fanciful links to Old Testament passages, but there's no doubt that the New Testament authors are happy to see Jesus' story as Israel's story. There are many parallels. Like the Israelites, Jesus comes out of Egypt (where his parents had fled) and like Israel, goes into the wilderness to be tempted by the devil. Joshua, the Hebrew name for Jesus, enters the promised land, depicting the rest into which Jesus leads us (Heb. 4). Jesus rules over a kingdom as the 'son of David', the Old Testament king who knew great victories over his enemies.

Jesus is the one who fulfils all the longings of His people as the perfect king, priest and prophet.

WEEK 3

Songs from the Heart

Opening Icebreaker

What would you select as a theme song for your life? Why did you choose it? Who would you want to sing it?

Bible Readings

- Psalm 103
- Psalm 42
- Psalm 51
- Psalm 19
- Psalm 2

Opening Our Eyes

The Psalms have been called 'Israel's hymn book' because they include many hymns and songs that were used in corporate, temple and personal worship in the life of Israel. Whereas most of Scripture can be said to speak *to* us, psalms typically speak *for* us, suggesting language to represent the wide range of emotions that we feel as we experience life's vicissitudes and address our praise and concerns to God.

Most psalms were written around the time of King David, who wrote seventy-three of the 150 Psalms and instituted a pattern of worship within the nation. The Psalter, however, can be seen as an 'open book' which had psalms added at various times in a 1,100-year period: fifty are anonymous, twelve are by Asaph, eleven by the Korahites, two by Solomon and one each by Moses and Ethan. A superscription appears on 117 of the Psalms. This may indicate a psalm's author, the circumstance in which it was written, or a musical notation.

Psalms are really Hebrew poetry, a genre of literature which also figures in other books: Job, Song of Songs, Ecclesiastes, parts of the prophets and occasionally in narrative books including, perhaps, the early chapters of Genesis. They are arranged in five books, possibly mirroring the five books of the law, although they have no organising theme.

Our understanding and interpretation of psalms is helped by considering some of the categories into which they have been grouped. Although scholars dispute how best to group them, most agree with the following broad categories, although some psalms will fit more than one category.

Praise Psalms

These are perhaps best known, because many contemporary hymns and songs are based on their words. They include: Psalms 8; 19:1–6; 33; 66:1–12; 67; 95; 100; 103; 104; 111; 113; 114; 117 and 145–150.

Praise psalms can be further subdivided into:

- covenant songs – psalms directed toward the covenant relationships between God and others (Psa. 50; 72:17–19; 78; 132)
- hymns of Zion/the Temple – psalms focused on Jerusalem, the place of God's presence (Psa. 46)
- royal psalms – these focus on the human king of Israel or upon God as King of Israel (Psa. 47)
- messianic psalms – those which attend to predictions concerning God's anointed representative who is yet to come, or the kingdom that He will rule (Psa. 2; 16).

Psalms of Lament

Many psalms express the pain and sadness of life. Some include shocking images – Psalm 137:9, for example, expresses joy if enemies of Israel see their infants' heads dashed against the rocks.

There are four types of lament: corporate (Psa. 12; 44), personal (Psa. 42; 43), repentance (Psa. 51) and imprecation (Psa. 137).

Wisdom Psalms

Wisdom psalms overlap topics found in the book of Proverbs. Contrasting the righteous and the wicked, they address God's blessings and cursing and often focus on righteous living (eg, Psa. 1; 5; 7; 9–12; 14–15).

Festival Psalms

Psalms 120 to 134 are known as 'The Songs of Ascents' or pilgrimage and are thought to have been sung by people as they approached the Temple in Jerusalem for the three

great festival periods of Passover, Pentecost and the Feast of Tabernacles. Psalms 113 to 118, known as 'hallel', are recited during the day of Passover. They are a celebration of the great acts of God in delivering His people from Egypt and they point forward to the deliverance that Jesus would bring.

Discussion Starters

1. Look at Psalm 103. What can you list as the benefits of knowing God?

2. Read Psalm 42. In this psalm, the psalmist has a conversation with himself. From noting the advice he gives himself, what might be a good way of dealing with times of personal despair?

3. Psalm 51 is clearly linked to David's repentance over his adultery with Bathsheba. How might his words in verses 1–12 be appropriate for us today?

4. Read Psalm 19 (a wisdom psalm) and consider the two kinds of revelation given. What does each do? Which affects you more?

_____

_____

_____

_____

_____

_____

5. Christians vary in their attitude to lament. What would be lost from our faith if there were no psalms of lament?

_____

_____

_____

_____

_____

6. Read Psalm 2, regarded as a messianic psalm. In the New Testament, the apostle Paul refers to this psalm in his speech in Acts 13:32–34. Why do you think the apostles felt the need to link the life of Jesus to the Old Testament?

_____

_____

_____

_____

_____

Personal Application

The Psalms provide inspiration as well as information, and, like much poetry, they move the heart as well as the mind. They are a reminder to more cerebral Christians that acknowledging and expressing emotion is a necessary part of the Christian's walk. Denial and suppression of emotion can be damaging to us – if we bury our emotions, they are buried alive and will come back to haunt us. Use the Psalms to give your emotions a work out, underlining verses that strike you because they are especially apt, and also those that surprise you.

Seeing Jesus in the Scriptures

Some scholars suggest that it is appropriate for many of the praise psalms to be sung and expressed to Jesus, who, as God become flesh, is worthy of the praise given to God. Certainly many modern chorus and song writers employ psalm language as love language that church congregations can use to express their love to Jesus.

Many of the Psalms express the rule of God over the whole world and over all the nations. At the time of their writing, this may have sounded ambitious: despite having subdued many of her enemies in the time of David, Israel was a small nation. But these psalms anticipate the reign of Jesus, the Messiah, the Son of David, who does indeed reign on David's throne today, whose kingdom does spread worldwide – a kingdom that, on His return, will one day finally be evident to all.

WEEK 4

God's Spokesmen

Opening Icebreaker

Has anyone in the group ever been on jury duty? Without going into detail, what kinds of cases were covered?

Bible Readings

- Amos 7:10–17
- Jeremiah 11:1–17
- Micah 6:1–8
- Isaiah 40:1–31
- Ezekiel 37:1–14
- Nahum 3:1–19

Opening Our Eyes

The role of the Old Testament prophets was to speak for
God, often at times of national trouble and crisis. They
reminded the kings and the people of their covenant
obligation to live as God had called them to, as a light
to the nations around – the purpose for which they
were rescued and called in Exodus 19. The prophets
were 'covenant enforcers' as they detailed for people the
laws that had been broken and the likelihood of God's
judgment if they didn't repent, including the ultimate
sanction of exclusion from the land of Canaan that God
had given them.

Of the hundreds of prophets in Israel, we have collections
of the sayings (oracles) of just sixteen, written between
760 BC and 460 BC and listed from Isaiah to Malachi
in the Old Testament. This is the period of the spiritual
decline of Israel (the ten tribes in the north) and Judah
(the two tribes in the south). The prophets reminded
both nations of the need to repent, though eventually
both were exiled from the land as a consequence of their
failure: Israel by the Assyrians in 722 BC and Judah by
the Babylonians in 586 BC. Messages are given to nations
close to Israel and Judah too: they are judged not because
they broke God's law (they didn't know it) but because
their behaviour violated their conscience.

The prophetic books are known by their timing in relation
to the Babylonian Exile (pre-exilic, exilic and post-
exilic). There is a little prophecy in the New Testament
– Jesus predicts the fall of Jerusalem, and Revelation is a
prophecy, though a different style from the Old Testament
books considered here.

Many read the prophets simply to spot the predictions
about Jesus, or speculate on what they say about the end
times. In fact, scholars suggest that less than two per cent

of Old Testament prophecy relates to Jesus, less than five percent specifically concerns the new covenant age and less than one per cent concern events still future to us.

Prophecy in Scripture is mostly *telling forth* God's Word, not simply *forth telling*. If we read the prophets in context they tell us of God's heart for His people and His desire that they display His love and goodness to the nations around. So our first clue to understanding this genre is to note *why* the prophet is telling forth! This is not always straightforward. In some cases, notably the longer books of Isaiah, Jeremiah and Ezekiel, the oracles are not arranged chronologically, and so it's not easy to spot the precise context of the message. Most readers need a Bible dictionary or commentary to discern the background to the book and individual oracles within that book.

Interpretation and application of a prophetic book go awry if we fail to realise that the prophet employs language appropriate to the message. All the prophetic books contain a substantial amount of poetry; several are exclusively poetic. Clearly the image of trees clapping their hands (Isa. 55:12) depicts creation rejoicing, but is not to be understood literally! Simile, metaphor, personification and hyperbole were used so that the hearers would appreciate God's feelings towards His people: His despair, anger, sadness, hope and joy. The prophets thus inspire our imaginations as well as inform our minds.

As with all Scripture we are wise to discern the message to the people in that day, and any future fulfilment in Scripture, before seeking to apply the message to our day.

Discussion Starters

1. Read Amos 7:10–17. This passage illustrates the way in which the prophet challenges both priests and kings in Israel. Can you see a role for this kind of prophet today?

_____

_____

_____

_____

_____

2. In Jeremiah 11:1–17 the warnings are pretty stark. Why do you think the message went unheeded by the people of Judah, especially as their northern neighbours, Israel, had already been exiled at this point? Why do people ignore God's warnings today?

_____

_____

_____

_____

_____

_____

3. Micah 6:1–8 uses the lawsuit style. Why is this style so powerful? How might you apply Micah 6:8 to your life?

_____

_____

_____

_____

_____

4. The images in Isaiah 40 speak of the return of Judah from Exile, and point forward to the coming of Jesus. List the pictures used. What comfort do you take from the passage?

_____

_____

_____

_____

_____

_____

5. Imagine the scene in Ezekiel 37. How is this image fulfilled in the new covenant?

_____

_____

_____

_____

_____

_____

6. Nahum prophesied to Nineveh some time after Jonah had preached there. What might Nahum 3 tell you about God's attitude to evil regimes?

_____

_____

_____

_____

_____

_____

Personal Application

The prophets open us up to the heart of God. In places they may seem very stern but they also include His gracious reminders to His people that they have strayed away from His commands. God waits hundreds of years before exile from the land finally comes.

God is also gentle and gracious with us. We too need to heed His Word to know blessing in our lives. Jesus said we would be His friends if we follow His commands (John 15:14). His Spirit will convict us of sin, as He seeks to develop godly character within us. Make it your aim to heed any warnings you receive from His Word and His Spirit today.

Seeing Jesus in the Scriptures

We have noted already that the prophets mainly speak of situations within Israel, Judah or the surrounding nations of that day. But they do also include predictions of the coming Messiah, Jesus, especially during and after the Exile when the people of God feared extinction. The whole Old Testament points towards the coming of Jesus, but in the prophets we have specific statements regarding His birth, genealogy, life, death and resurrection, ascension, and present role at the helm of the universe. The New Testament authors are keen to point out how Jesus fulfils what the prophets had promised and indeed how He had exceeded their expectations. This is a powerful apologetic – does it not seem likely that our Bible is divinely inspired? What other book includes writings which predict the future with such accuracy?

WEEK 5

One Gospel: Four Accounts

Opening Icebreaker

Recall an event of which you were all part. It might be the previous study, a social event, or even the beginning of this meeting. What differences are there between your accounts? Are there any disagreements over what happened?

Bible Readings

- Mark 1:9–45; 2:1–28
- John 2:1–10
- Matthew 13:31–52
- John 15:1–8
- Luke 24:13–35
- Matthew 28:18–20

Opening Our Eyes

The Gospels are some of the best known but least understood documents in the Bible. Best known, because they include familiar stories of the birth, life, death and resurrection of Jesus, detailing His teaching, miracles and the calling of people to follow Him. But least understood because they are not typically read as they were written: namely as documents aiming to serve communities aware of, and interested in, the good news of the coming of Jesus. As a result many know the stories without knowing the specific style of writing employed by the four authors and why they arranged their material as they did.

It's useful to consider some of the words used to describe the gospel genre:

Biography

The Gospels clearly have biographical elements. But they are not the kind of biographies written today. Only two show any interest in Jesus' birth, only one story occurs before His public ministry, and the majority of the material comes from the last week of Jesus' life. Most biographical questions are left unanswered.

History

Luke claims, both in the prologue to his Gospel (Luke 1:1–4) and the prologue to (Acts 1:3), to be writing history based on eyewitness accounts of the events. The tradition that Mark wrote his Gospel based on the preaching of Peter suggests that Mark did base his Gospel on the personal testimony of Peter. Mark appears to be used by both Matthew and Luke, Matthew also being an eyewitness. The writer of the fourth Gospel supplements this material with further eyewitness testimony, albeit from a theological angle at a much later date.

Theology

In John 20:30–31, the author of the fourth Gospel states that his purpose was to convince the readers of a theological fact, that '... Jesus is the Messiah, the Son of God ...' and that by believing this theology, the reader might '... have life in his name'.

While John's Gospel is the most theological of the four, Matthew, Mark and Luke have clear theological agendas. You cannot approach these documents without getting into the question of who Jesus is, who He claims to be, and how the gospel writers present Him in their telling of the story.

So we might conclude that the Gospels are *theological biographies*. The accounts are presented through a theological grid as the writers select material from the events of Jesus' life which make a theological point. In particular, they show that Jesus is the Son of God, that He is fully human and that He died as an atoning sacrifice for mankind.

Because of their use of common sources, the Gospels of Matthew, Mark and Luke are known as synoptic Gospels. They were probably written around the time of the fall of Jerusalem in AD 70, when it was thought necessary to commit to parchment the many stories and accounts of the life of Jesus circulating within the Christian communities in Judea and throughout the Roman world. John's Gospel is possibly written later, although probably before AD 90. Scholars have various theories about the intended audiences for the Gospels, but it seems likely that Matthew probably wrote with a Jewish audience in mind, and Luke a Gentile one.

Discussion Starters

1. Mark demonstrates who Jesus is in the opening to his Gospel. Scan the topics in Mark 1:9–45 and 2:1–28. Over what does he claim that Jesus is Lord?

2. Read John 2:1–10. John arranges his material around seven signs (miracles), of which this is the first. What does this sign tell us about Jesus?

3. Look at Matthew 13:31–52. These parables are unique to Matthew. What do they tell us about the kind of kingdom that Jesus was bringing?

4. The radical words of Jesus in John 15:1–8 suggest that we now go to Him to connect with God, rather than through Israel as in the old covenant. How can you remain close to Jesus?

_____

_____

_____

_____

_____

_____

5. Read Luke 24:13–35. This resurrection appearance is unique to Luke. What points of humour can you see in the story?

_____

_____

_____

_____

_____

_____

6. Read Matthew 28:18–20. Some believe that Matthew has arranged his Gospel as a teaching manual. What do Jesus' words imply about the way in which Christians are to grow?

_____

_____

_____

_____

_____

_____

Personal Application

It may seem clear that the Gospels automatically relate to us today. Certainly most of His teaching to the Twelve can be applied to us as followers of Jesus, especially if we take Matthew 28:18–20 seriously. The Gospels provide us with the message that the apostles preached and which we are to preach today: the availability of the rule and reign of God for all who would learn from Jesus how to live. We embrace His lifestyle of denying self, taking up our cross, and following Him. This is the easy yoke and life of peace Jesus promises to those who embrace His way. We should also expect God to intervene in our world as we look to Him in prayer for our needs and those of others.

Seeing Jesus in the Scriptures

It is not hard to see Jesus in the Gospels! But do we see Him as He is, or as we expect Him to be? Too often Jesus has been divorced from His context, and made to wear the colours of a national or political agenda. Jesus was a Jew fully conversant with the Old Testament Law, faithful in attending synagogue and adopting the regulations and festivals of the Jews. Yet at the same time He challenged what the Jewish faith had become, showing that inner transformation is needed to embrace the spirit and not just the letter of the Law. He came to die for His people first, becoming the answer to Israel's longing for forgiveness and peace, even as His death also became the means for all nations to come to know God. He came to show how we can live as those born of the same Spirit that anointed Him.

WEEK 6

Special Correspondence

Opening Icebreaker

Set up a mobile phone conversation between two people, one in the room and one outside. The latter person is shopping for a watch for their father's sixtieth birthday. Without mentioning the word 'watch', the first person needs to find out as much as possible about the search. This demonstrates the difficulty of understanding something from hearing just one side of a conversation. Can anyone in the group work out what was happening?

Bible Readings

- Galatians 3:1–14
- Ephesians 2:1–10
- Philippians 4:1–9
- 1 Timothy 4:1–16
- James 1:1–7
- 2 Peter 1:3–11

Opening Our Eyes

At first glance, the Epistles seem to be some of the easiest documents to understand and interpret in the whole Bible. Although written letters are becoming less popular in our electronic age we understand the concept of an individual (typically an apostle) writing to a church or individual. What could be simpler? In some cases this is exactly what we have: the Epistles are documents written by Paul and other apostles and church leaders who felt the need to explain the Christian faith in writing in the light of the challenges that churches and individuals were facing in the decades following the ascension of Jesus. They are listed after the book of Acts in the New Testament, with the Epistles believed to have been written by Paul first, followed by the rest. Paul's letters and Hebrews are given the title of the recipients; the rest are known by the name of the assumed author. An epistle was generally a response to a live issue or issues, not a reasoned theological treatise. Indeed, in the apostle Paul's case, four were written from prison, probably in Rome. In the case of some of the Pauline Epistles (thirteen were attributed to him) we can cross reference the epistle to incidents recorded in Acts and grasp some of the background that may inform the letter.

But if some of the Epistles are relatively straightforward in this respect, others are less so and the reading of an epistle has been rightly likened to listening to one side of a phone conversation. It is not always clear why the apostle is choosing to address an issue, or why he addresses it in a certain way and scholars have spilt much ink seeking to give their explanations. Furthermore, in some of the Epistles, such as 1, 2 and 3 John we do not know for sure why or when the letter was written; in the case of Hebrews there is no real consensus amongst scholars about who wrote it.

If understanding can be tricky, the application of texts drawn from the Epistles also requires careful handling – a principle we have often addressed in these studies. We must understand which aspects of each letter were appropriate for that day and that culture, then decide which aspects are timeless principles which relate to us today. For example, Paul's request that a cloak be brought to him (2Tim. 4:13) was clearly for there and then, but what of the command that women be silent in church (1Cor. 14:34–35)? If enforced, this command would mean that only men sing hymns and choruses – but no church adopts this practice today.

So the Epistles are not as straightforward as we might imagine – they contain some of the most profound theology and heart-warming truth found anywhere in Scripture. Paul's epistles typically start with a reminder of what God has done for those who trust in Christ before going on to exhort them to live godly lives. Peter's epistles outline how we can trust in God in the face of suffering. Hebrews demonstrates how Christ is so wonderfully superior to the old covenant; John challenges us to love one another while James provides pithy advice for all seasons of life. For this reason, the study of the Epistles is a staple diet for many churches, equipping and inspiring God's people as they seek to understand what following Christ in the power of the Spirit is really about.

Discussion Starters

1. In Galatians 3:1–14 Paul expresses his anger to the Galatians. Why is he cross and what application might this have for Christians today?

_____

_____

_____

_____

_____

_____

2. List the negative and positive words in Ephesians 2:1–10. Does anything strike you in particular?

_____

_____

_____

_____

_____

_____

3. Read Philippians 4:1–9. Which of these exhortations are for you to apply to your life and which are for the first-century Christians?

_____

_____

_____

_____

_____

_____

4. Look at 1 Timothy 4:1–16. How do we discern whether these exhortations to Timothy are also to be practised by us today?

_____

_____

_____

_____

_____

_____

5. Read James 1:1–7. Do you consider trials 'pure joy'? What mind set is encouraged in this passage?

_____

_____

_____

_____

_____

_____

6. In 2 Peter 1:3–11, what is God's work and what is ours? How might you put this into practice?

_____

_____

_____

_____

_____

_____

Personal Application

God chose to birth His Word within the ups and downs of real life and real situations. After the ascension, He didn't send an angel to gather the apostles in order to lay down how the Church should function. Instead, His Spirit led His people to make Christ known and inspired individual people to write letters, dealing with things as they went.

You can trust the same Spirit to lead and guide you. Each day you will face issues not specifically mentioned in the Bible. Allow the Bible and wise Christians to train you in the discernment of any biblical principles which apply to you. Then trust God to help you navigate through life in a way that blesses those around you and brings glory to Him.

Seeing Jesus in the Scriptures

The apostle Paul urges his readers to know the reality of a life 'in Christ'. It is true that Christ dwells in our hearts by His Spirit, but it is the theme of us 'in Christ' that was so often precious to Paul. This idea implies security: we are connected to the One who is the Lord of all, and Saviour of all who will come to Him. It also implies power: we are enabled to live in His grace. We may battle with sin, but this is not who we are: we are raised with Christ in heavenly places; we are to set our minds on things above. We have a glorious calling and it is from this position that we live. John would later urge his readers that whoever claims to live in God must walk as Jesus did. The Epistles are a wonderful treasure for us as we aim to emulate those who established what living in Christ looked like in the early decades after Jesus' earthly life.

WEEK 7

Cracking Ancient Code

Opening Icebreaker

Which of these acronyms do you know?

FAQ	WWF
KFC	HTTP
ATM	SCUBA
DVD	ADHD
CD-ROM	FIFA

How many of these acronyms would make any sense to a first-century person?

Bible Readings

- Daniel 7:1–28
- Ezekiel 40:3–4; 43:1–12
- Zechariah 1:7–20
- Revelation 7:1–17
- Revelation 16:1–21
- Revelation 21:1–8

Opening Our Eyes

If you have ever spent time trying to read the book of Revelation (especially chapter 4 onwards), you will know that it is a whole different ball game to other literature we have considered. There are animals, mythical monsters, angels and humans in extraordinary settings. Its style suggests mystery and it's no surprise that Revelation has become a playground for aspiring code breakers with fertile imaginations.

This style is known as apocalyptic, a word taken from the Greek term *apokalypsis*, used in Revelation 1:1. It means 'unveiling' or 'revelation' and is used to describe literature included in some of the Old Testament prophets: parts of Ezekiel, Joel, Amos, Zechariah and large parts of Daniel. It was a style used outside the Bible during the period 200 BC – 100 AD which has similarities with prophecy. But whereas prophecy was written to people in need of repentance, apocalyptic literature was written to people in need of reassurance. It was used to encourage the people of God during traumatic times – often persecution. It is thought that its esoteric language may have been understood by the readers but written off by their persecutors as idle nonsense, while its graphic language aims to convey the seriousness of the message – shouting to the reader, 'This matters. Pay attention!'

In the book of Revelation some of its symbolism is taken directly from the Old Testament, with imagery and metaphors adapted and used as material for graphic figurative representation. It's no surprise to learn that interpreting such literature is tricky; most readers will need a Bible commentary to explore the text and reach a view on the author's intentions.

Be aware that scholars and Bible teachers differ in their approaches, especially when it comes to the book of

Revelation. How you read and interpret the book will be governed by which of the following methods you use:

- The Preterist method believes that all the events took place within the period of time that is contemporary to the writer, ie first century AD
- the Futurist method states that all of the recorded events in the text have yet to take place
- the Historicist method suggests that events described in the text are directly related to world events that can range from the time of the writer to the end of the age
- the Idealist method does not tie the events of apocalyptic literature to either historical or future events, but searches for the author's intended spiritual meaning.

This study favours the preterist view that the book is written to encourage Christians facing persecution in the first century AD. It assures them of the victory of God over all powers set against Him. But some of the events are clearly still to take place: we still await the new heaven and earth in the final chapters.

Our reading of apocalyptic literature in the two testaments will be aided by remembering the following:

- the hero often takes a journey, accompanied by an angelic messenger who shows him interesting sights and comments on them
- the visions use strange, even enigmatic, symbolism
- the visions are shocking, and often pessimistic about the hope for a human solution to the situation
- at the end, God's brings the present state of affairs to an end with a better situation
- the writer often takes past history and rewrites it as if it were prophecy
- apocalyptic writing focuses on comforting and sustaining the 'righteous remnant' (Isa.10:20–22).

Discussion Starters

1. Look at the four beasts in Daniel 7:1–28. What do
    these represent? What becomes of the servants of the
    Most High? How would you feel if you were facing
    persecution and read this passage?

    _____
    _____
    _____
    _____
    _____

2. Read Ezekiel 40:3–4 and 43:1–12. The people are
    in exile hundreds of miles from home. How is God
    encouraging His people through this vision?

    _____
    _____
    _____
    _____
    _____

3. Read Zechariah 1:7–20. This book was written at a
    time when rebuilding the Temple seemed a tough
    task. How would these words have helped the people
    to work?

    _____
    _____
    _____
    _____
    _____

4. Read Revelation 7:1–17. What do you think the symbolism is intended to convey?

_____

_____

_____

_____

_____

_____

5. How might the language of Revelation 16:1–21 encourage Christians facing persecution? How do you balance this language with God's love?

_____

_____

_____

_____

_____

6. How does the vision in Revelation 21:1–8 contrast with the assumption of some Christians that we go to heaven? How do you understand this passage?

_____

_____

_____

_____

_____

Personal Application

The Bible includes all of life – the joy and the pain. Apocalyptic literature reminds us that God does not keep His people from suffering, but does provide encouragement so that His people do not lose heart or faith during it. Whether you are presently struggling, or not, this literature reminds us that God will one day bring an end to pain and suffering and in the meantime He gives us strength to endure, including reminders that relief will come one day. What is eternity with God compared to the present trial?

Seeing Jesus in the Scriptures

Daniel 7 is believed to be the backdrop to understanding why Jesus uses the enigmatic term 'Son of Man' to refer to Himself. It identifies Him with our humanity, but also speaks of this special figure who is given: '… authority, glory and sovereign power; all peoples, nations and men of every language worshipped him. His dominion is an everlasting dominion that will not pass away, and his kingdom is one that will never be destroyed' (v.14).

The book of Revelation comes '… from Jesus Christ, which God gave him to show his servants what must soon take place. He made it known by sending his angel to his servant John …' (Rev. 1:1).

We see a vision of Jesus in the opening chapter and references to Him in Revelation 5 as a sacrificial Lamb, as '… the Lion of the tribe of Judah, the Root of David …' (v.5) and one of the concluding visions of the Apocalypse pictures the victorious 'King of kings, and Lord of lords', riding triumphantly on a white horse – a symbol of conquest (Rev. 19:11–16).

Leader's Notes

Week 1: The Right Side of the Law

Hopefully, this is a fun introduction to the way some laws and rules function. Often laws will seem odd because we don't understand their context. Some of the laws in the Old Testament seem odd to western eyes because they were written for a people in a different culture and day to our own.

Aim of the Session
The aim of this session is to see how we can interpret Old Testament laws in the light of the new covenant and thus give examples of the approach taken in the Bible.

Discussion Starters
2: This question demonstrates that many of the so-called 'restrictions' of the Ten Commandments are commands that people generally regard as sensible. We want to live in a society where no one will take our life, our possessions, or our spouse, or have a covetous attitude to us for what we own. We want good relationships with our children and to have at least one day off a week. We don't want people to tell lies about us. Of course, few see that the early commands about putting God first are important, or that His priority gives us the ability to follow through on the rest.

In a covenant the greater party, in this case God, promises protection for and blessing of the lesser part, Israel, providing the covenant obligations (laws) are met. The laws function as a way of reminding future generations of where they have come from. Note especially how their obedience is linked to blessing.

3: All the ceremonial and sacrificial laws reflect a need for the people to live in communion with God. The punishments for law breakers clarify the seriousness of sin and this passage describes how both the community and the leaders would have known the gravity of misdemeanour.

In his epistle, John reminds us that we can know forgiveness in Jesus (1 John 1:8–9). But the New Testament also reminds us that we work out our salvation with fear and trembling (Phil. 2:12–13). Just because we no longer have to go through animal sacrifice, sin still matters – it grieves God's Spirit and diminishes our capacity to love and worship Him. Left unchecked and unforgiven it will draw us away from God.

4: The warnings in Deuteronomy 17 were not heeded and the kings of Israel behaved as predicted, most notably Solomon who effectively enslaved the people (1 Kings 9: 20–23), multiplied horses (1 Kings 10:26) and was enticed by women to worship foreign gods (1 Kings 11:1–8).

5: The system of law in Israel was an enlightened and liberating one within those days, suggesting a 'fairness' that many peoples would later acknowledge when framing their own legislation – notably English law.

The laws did not account for every eventuality but many of the laws gave principles that could then be applied to other situations, rather as case law is used today.

6: This passage gives us an appropriate attitude to the Law in the Old Testament. We are grateful for the guidance it gives us, but also for the One who frees us from its demands.

Week 2: God tells a Good Story

Opening Icebreaker
Most in the study will enjoy stories and this aims
to get people talking about the wonder of narrative
communication.

Aim of the Session
The aim is to give a glimpse of the ways in which the
editors and writers of the Bible tell stories through God's
inspiration. You don't have time to do justice to the meta-
narrative of course, but the questions aim to bring out
the skilful way in which the narrators make their points
through the medium of story, whilst entertaining and
intriguing us as well.

Discussion Starters
1 and 2: The Old Testament narrative is formed around the
idea of God fulfilling His promise. It establishes that God is
good and promises to bless His people. So the patriarchs,
Abraham, Isaac and Jacob are people who become gripped
by God's promise, which is fulfilled in spite of their own
personal failings and circumstances, notably childlessness,
which seem to contradict the promise.

The Israelites are in Egypt 400 years before they cry
out to God again. Moses is reminded that he stands in
the flow of God's intentions to bless Abraham and his
descendants.

3 and 4: You can hopefully have fun imagining David and
Goliath on screen.

It's trickier, however, to think about the role of the story
in the book of Samuel as part of Israel's bigger story. In
it, we have King Saul who had been rejected by God, and
the young man anointed to be king but not yet crowned,
and who would not be crowned for some years. So we

have a man who should be leading and demonstrating God's power who is impoverished, and a man, David, who is empowered to serve, having developed his trust in God in the secret places when guarding sheep.

This story sets the stage for what will follow: Saul's hunting of David and his sad end, and David's development, as a hero in Israel, to be the greatest king they ever had.

5: In Acts we have an example of a repeated idea, showing how the growth of the Word and the Church happened as God's kingdom advanced across the Roman Empire. Knowledge of the broad direction of Acts helps us interpret the individual stories that Luke includes. For example, why is Philip moved from a thriving situation to meet one travelling eunuch? It demonstrates how the Gospel comes to Ethiopia.

Luke is an expert historian and storyteller as he marshals his research to show how God fulfils His commands in Acts 1:8, in spite of the apostles' initial reluctance to move. The book tells us many things, notably the way the message of Jesus was proclaimed as it encountered different people groups. But it is never less than the glorious story of how twelve men turned the Roman world upside down.

Week 3: Songs from the Heart

Opening Icebreaker
The icebreaker tries to tap into the way contemporary songs so often speak to us and for us. They express the emotions we feel. This thought helps to introduce the idea of songs and hymns that speak for us, or perhaps give us words for what we would like to be true, but which isn't yet true.

Aim of the Session

The readings aim to give a flavour of the wide range of psalms, and in particular to see that they are not just about praise. Most local churches' diet of psalm-based songs and hymns might give that impression. The nickname, 'happy clappy' was not coined for nothing!

Discussion Starters

1: It's important that this question is not seen as merely a comprehension exercise. Do we really believe that the benefits listed are ours too?

2: This question aims to help people to express how we might deal with darker times in our lives. You might find the discussion flows easily, but some church cultures make it less easy to talk about personal despair. The psalmists do not flinch from speaking about pain and we need to get into the habit of doing so if we are to truly engage with God. So be prepared to be provocative as you gauge the mood of the meeting and get people talking.

3: Imagine thousands of people singing about your personal failure! Yet this psalm does just that. It has given voice to countless saints down through history and whatever our church affiliation or practice, it can be usefully used today. The group can, of course, talk in general terms without having to be personal themselves, unless this is appropriate.

4: Psalm 19 gives us examples of *general* revelation (the world around) and *special* revelation (the Word of God) here exemplified by the Law. We need to pay attention to both. The group may feel obliged to respond that the law of God affects them more, but the reality is that the natural world also does something to us: a summer's day, lush green grass, fields of colourful flowers and majestic snow-topped mountains all speak of God. It's no disgrace for us to delight in them as they point to the Creator.

5: Here we look at the legitimacy of crying out to God because of what has happened. It's healthy physically and spiritually to give voice to our responses and the Psalms give us license to do so, if we need it. If laments didn't exist, wouldn't we be tempted to suppress our emotion and assume that God is not concerned?

6: For the Jews to accept Jesus as the Messiah, they needed to see that He really did fulfil Old Testament prophecy. The apostles were keen to urge their readers and listeners to understand the Old Testament in the light of Christ, as the One of whom the Scriptures spoke. Such verses are a bit like Jesus' CV – they outline His right to the role of Messiah, albeit in a different way to how the Jews had expected.

Week 4: God's Spokesmen

Opening Icebreaker

The icebreaker alludes to the prophets' role as covenant enforcers, although the analogy of the lawyer can be taken too far. The prophets in Israel acted a little like lawyers in a court of law. On occasions they 'saw the future' but more often their job was to interpret the present and show Israel and Judah how they had failed to follow the Law and what the consequences of disobedience would be. Unlike a prosecuting lawyer, they do offer hope – the Judge (God) is actually on their side and will not give up on them.

Aim of the Session

This session aims to introduce various kinds of prophecy, underlining the idea that prophets *tell forth* far more than they *forth tell*.

Discussion Starters

1: This gives a great insight into the prophetic role. Some see the Church as having a prophetic role in society. Others believe they can bring God's Word to those in authority. This may be true; certainly it's generally true that church leaders should not have political power, but we need to be careful before jumping straight from Amos to parliament. The prophets' position in relation to the nation of Israel in covenant with God is different from that of those gifted as prophets who are in nations not under covenant in that same way, even if the country in question is nominally Christian, such as the UK.

2: It's worth remembering two dates: the exile of the northern tribes (Israel) in 722 BC and the exile of the southern tribes (Judah) in 586 BC. The northern tribes were dispersed among the nations and never returned to the land. Judah was able to return seventy years later.

5: The prophets want us to use our imagination. You may want to read the passage out loud and have people imagine it with their eyes shut. Read it slowly so that people have time to paint the picture in their minds. This coming of the Spirit is fulfilled at Pentecost. Israel as a nation went into Exile never to return. Judah would return to the land so there was never any physical reuniting of the two nations. The coming of the Spirit means that all, wherever they are, Judah, the lost tribes of Israel and all the nations of the earth, can become one in the Church of Jesus Christ.

6: We know that Nahum prophesied around 663 BC. The date of Jonah's prophecy to the people of Nineveh was earlier; though we don't know the date for sure it may have been around 760 BC. You may recall that Jonah was upset that Nineveh repented because he was so angry with their behaviour and wanted God to judge them. In Nahum he gets his wish! You may wonder why God allows evil regimes to prosper today – Nahum reminds us that God will act eventually.

Week 5: One Gospel: Four Accounts

Opening Icebreaker

The four Gospels provide four windows on the life of Jesus. The accounts are different, but not contradictory. Just as group members will have different recollections about a common event, so the Evangelists (as the gospel writers are known) write based on their eyewitness accounts (their own or others). Together they provide a God-inspired portrait of Jesus.

Aim of the Session

The aim of this session is to gain a sense of the different approaches taken by the gospel (good news) writers. There is really one Gospel! Each writer provides *The Gospel According to* … and I have chosen passages unique to each gospel writer. There's no space here to unpack the individual approaches that each takes. A good commentary on the Gospels would explore this fascinating theme in more depth.

Discussion Starters

1: Jesus is Lord over: Satan; those following Him; impure spirits; fever; various diseases; leprosy; paralysis and Jewish regulations, including behaviour on the Sabbath.

Jesus clearly challenges society with a new way of understanding life, based on the power of God.

2: This seems to be an insignificant wedding and an unusual miracle because no one's life is at stake! Jesus is happy to save the day, and in so doing provides an abundance of wine. You can calculate that the jars would hold 150 gallons, 682 litres or 900 bottles! The sign can be understood for its spiritual significance. Elsewhere in the Gospels, Jesus describes His teaching and ministry as new wine, requiring new wineskins. When He says, 'I am the true vine …' (John 15:1), this is a clear reference to the failure of Israel (depicted in the Old Testament as being like a vine) to produce fruit. We are to gain our nourishment and life from Him.

3: This passage is one of many which illustrate how Jesus came to be what Israel failed to be: a light to the nations and a blessing to all peoples. It was very radical teaching for people who revered the nation and its institutions.

4: The metaphor of remaining in the vine needs teasing out. The passage speaks of obeying Jesus' teaching as a key element. It's worth pressing people to provide specific ways that they might stay close to God. This may include private prayer, prayer with others, times of solitude and silence, fasting and private and corporate worship.

5: Note in particular Jesus' comment, 'What things?' (v.19). He had been involved in redeeming the world though His death on the cross and yet He nonchalantly asks, 'What things?' When His companions arrive at their home, He pretends to go on – like He had somewhere to go!

6: This passage, containing the words recited at baptisms, is commonly misunderstood as being about mission. The passage actually says that as we go we are to make disciples (going may be across the street or across the world). The command is to immerse people in the Trinitarian life of God; it's not focusing on the words said at baptisms. We will surely need empowering to serve the world in this way.

But the key area to underline is that we are to teach everything that Jesus commanded, implying that His character and behaviour in demonstrating the kingdom of God was to be the approach of these followers and, indeed, those who would come after Him.

Week 6: Special Correspondence

Opening Icebreaker
The icebreaker demonstrates that we sometimes read the Epistles unaware of the precise reason why particular areas were covered. It's like listening to one side of a phone conversation. Our job is to grasp the essentials as best we can.

Aim of the Session
The aim of the session is to examine what the Epistles are and to consider that applying them to life today is not always straightforward.

Discussion Starters
1: This passage demonstrates one of the apostle Paul's key battlegrounds as he explains Christian faith to Jews and Gentiles. Elsewhere in his letters, he explains the preciousness of the law of God. But we see the law today in the light of Jesus who fully keeps the law's requirements. If we attempt to keep the law, it will drive us crazy and Paul feared that the Galatians might miss the joy and peace that comes from knowing that we are justified before God because of Jesus.

3: We can typically read a passage from an epistle and assume that it all applies directly. Although we need to remember that the Bible was not written *to* us but *for* us, most of this passage will, in fact, translate. The specific comment to Euodia and Syntyche won't apply directly, but it illustrates the principle of working through differences. We don't know for sure what the problem was between these two women, but doubtless it was a bit embarrassing for them to find the apostle bringing up the matter in a publicly read letter. Make sure people reflect on how they would take the exhortations of this passage to heart.

4: This question is not intended to trigger an in-depth discussion about the finer points of the passage – you won't have time for that. But it is intended to help the group appreciate that in the first instance this was a letter written by the apostle to his younger, trusted friend who had been sent to Ephesus to provide stability at a difficult time. He had a particular role – probably more as an apostolic emissary than as a pastor in the sense that we might use the word today, and so we have to note that before jumping to conclusions. That said, we are still in the 'last days' (these being the period between Christ's first and second coming) and it's wise for us to grow and learn from God through the Scriptures. And if there are preachers present, what a great exhortation to keep working!

6: The passage clearly illustrates a principle that is explored in many of the Epistles in the New Testament. God is wonderfully at work in our lives, but we have to expend effort ourselves. The grace of God is not infused into us and we need to do things in response to what God has called us to be. These are not 'works' that we practise to save us, but actions that reflect a life that has been saved, is being saved and will be saved on the last day.

Urge the group to reflect on what 'making every effort' might look like practically and what might be a realistic aim for the coming week.

Week 7: Cracking Ancient Code

Opening Icebreaker

The icebreaker seeks to show that just as we have modern codes that are known and understood in relevant circles, so apocalyptic language would have been understood at the time it was written, even if we may struggle to understand it today.

Here are the answers:
FAQ: frequently asked questions
KFC: Kentucky Fried Chicken
ATM: automated teller machine
DVD: this was originally an acronym of the unofficial term digital video disk, but is now stated by the DVD Forum as standing for Digital Versatile Disc
CD-ROM: Compact Disc read-only memory
WWF: originally stood for World Wildlife Fund, but now stands for Worldwide Fund for Nature (although the former name is still used in the US)
HTTP: Hypertext Transfer Protocol
SCUBA: self-contained underwater breathing apparatus
ADHD: attention deficit-hyperactivity disorder
FIFA: football's governing body Fédération Internationale de Football Association

Aim of the Session

The aim of the session is to look at some of the books that use apocalyptic language and tease out how they may be understood, especially the book of Revelation.

Discussion Starters

1: Some apocalyptic language includes a degree of explanation; if members of the group read on they will find a partial answer, though which kings they represent are not specified. To interpret this passage it is key that we realise that the 'son of man' coming on the clouds of heaven is almost certainly a reference to Jesus' ascension, not his second coming. The passage teaches that God's people will eventually be vindicated and victorious because of the Son of man, though they wouldn't, of course, have known at that stage how God intended to fulfil His purpose.

3: According to Zechariah 1:1,7 and 7:1, Zechariah prophesied around 520–518 BC. The book can be thought of as a sequel to Haggai's book which had encouraged the people to rebuild the Temple. It had been destroyed by the Babylonians in 586 BC and not rebuilt when the people of Judah returned to the land in 538 BC. They had done nothing to the Temple in two decades, and had received criticism and threats from their opponents who inhabited Jerusalem and the surrounding area and who didn't want the rebuilding to take place.

4: Admittedly, this is a tricky and disputed passage. Jehovah's Witnesses make this a pivotal passage in their view of the afterlife. But careful reading and reflection by the group might reveal that the vision symbolises the unity between the people of God in the Old Testament and those from the nations who come to faith in New Testament times.

These were troubled times and this passage assures them that all will be well in the world to come.

5: This may be a tough chapter to read. It reads like a sci-fi adventure in which the villain has the upper hand. Please do not try and interpret each bowl, and Armageddon is not an end-time venue for the last battle. Note instead that the writer is using imagery from the judgment of Egypt in Exodus 10:21–29. Most of Revelation is interpreted through an understanding of the Old Testament. The implication from this passage is that God is all powerful – just as Pharaoh remained hardened to the wrath of God in his time, the evil authorities confronting Christians at this time will not necessarily bow to Jesus in the short term. But in the end, God will be victorious (vv.17,19).

6: Some may be alarmed at this question – don't we go to heaven when we die? It is clear that those who trust in Christ go to heaven when they die. But heaven is not a location in a far off distant galaxy, but a waiting room for the consummation of all things when, as depicted here, God restores all things to a new heaven and earth. This vision shows us that God is not finished with this earth, but will judge and remove all sin, and provide us with new bodies equipped for the new experience. God is coming back to earth!

National Distributors

UK: (and countries not listed below)

CWR, Waverley Abbey House, Waverley Lane, Farnham, Surrey GU9 8EP.
Tel: (01252) 784700 Outside UK (44) 1252 784700 Email: mail@cwr.org.uk

AUSTRALIA: KI Entertainment, Unit 21 317-321 Woodpark Road, Smithfield, New South Wales 2164.
Tel: 1 800 850 777 Fax: 02 9604 3699 Email: sales@kientertainment.com.au

CANADA: David C Cook Distribution Canada, PO Box 98, 55 Woodslee Avenue, Paris, Ontario N3L 3E5.
Tel: 1800 263 2664 Email: sandi.swanson@davidccook.ca

GHANA: Challenge Enterprises of Ghana, PO Box 5723, Accra.
Tel: (021) 222437/223249 Fax: (021) 226227 Email: ceg@africaonline.com.gh

HONG KONG: Cross Communications Ltd, 1/F, 562A Nathan Road, Kowloon.
Tel: 2780 1188 Fax: 2770 6229 Email: cross@crosshk.com

INDIA: Crystal Communications, 10-3-18/4/1, East Marredpalli, Secunderabad – 500026, Andhra
Pradesh. Tel/Fax: (040) 27737145 Email: crystal_edwj@rediffmail.com

KENYA: Keswick Books and Gifts Ltd, PO Box 10242-00400, Nairobi. Tel: (020) 2226047/312639
Email: sales.keswick@africaonline.co.ke

MALAYSIA: Canaanland Distributors Sdn Bhd, No. 25 Jalan PJU 1A/41B, NZX Commercial Centre,
Ara Jaya, 47301 Petaling Jaya, Selangor. Tel: (03) 7885 0540/1/2 Fax: (03) 7885 0545
Email: info@canaanland.com.my

Salvation Publishing & Distribution Sdn Bhd, 23 Jalan SS 2/64, 47300 Petaling Jaya, Selangor.
Tel: (03) 78766411/78766797 Fax: (03) 78757066/78756360 Email: info@salvationbookcentre.com

NEW ZEALAND: KI Entertainment, Unit 21 317-321 Woodpark Road, Smithfield, New South Wales
2164, Australia. Tel: 0 800 850 777 Fax: +612 9604 3699 Email: sales@kientertainment.com.au

NIGERIA: FBFM, Helen Baugh House, 96 St Finbarr's College Road, Akoka, Lagos.
Tel: (01) 7747429/4700218/825775/827264 Email: fbfm_1@yahoo.com

PHILIPPINES: OMF Literature Inc, 776 Boni Avenue, Mandaluyong City. Tel: (02) 531 2183
Fax: (02) 531 1960 Email: gloadlaon@omflit.com

SINGAPORE: Alby Commercial Enterprises Pte Ltd, 95 Kallang Avenue #04-00, AIS Industrial
Building, 339420. Tel: (65) 629 27238 Fax: (65) 629 27235 Email: marketing@alby.com.sg

SRI LANKA: Christombu Publications (Pvt) Ltd, Bartleet House, 65 Braybrooke Place, Colombo 2.
Tel: (9411) 2421073/2447665 Email: christombupublications@gmail.com

USA: David C Cook Distribution Canada, PO Box 98, 55 Woodslee Avenue, Paris, Ontario N3L 3E5,
Canada. Tel: 1800 263 2664 Email: sandi.swanson@davidccook.ca

CWR is a Registered Charity - Number 294387
CWR is a Limited Company registered in England - Registration Number 1990308

Courses and seminars

Publishing and new media

Conference facilities

Transforming lives

CWR's vision is to enable people to experience personal transformation through applying God's Word to their lives and relationships.

Our Bible-based training and resources help people around the world to:
- Grow in their walk with God
- Understand and apply Scripture to their lives
- Resource themselves and their church
- Develop pastoral care and counselling skills
- Train for leadership
- Strengthen relationships, marriage and family life and much more.

Our insightful writers provide daily Bible-reading notes and other resources for all ages, and our experienced course designers and presenters have gained an international reputation for excellence and effectiveness.

CWR's Training and Conference Centres in Surrey and East Sussex, England, provide excellent facilities in idyllic settings – ideal for both learning and spiritual refreshment.

 Applying God's Word
to everyday life and relationships

CWR, Waverley Abbey House,
Waverley Lane, Farnham,
Surrey GU9 8EP, UK

Telephone: **+44 (0)1252 784700**
Email: **info@cwr.org.uk**
Website: **www.cwr.org.uk**

Registered Charity No 294387
Company Registration No 1990308

Dramatic new resource

Daniel - Living boldly for God
by Christine Platt

Discover how Daniel lived boldly for God in a hostile culture and consider his extreme courage in a crisis. Reflect on how we can apply what we learn as we seek to live boldly for God in our own lives.

72-page booklet, 210x148mm
ISBN: 978-1-85345-986-3

The bestselling *Cover to Cover* Bible Study Series

1 Corinthians
Growing a Spirit-filled church
ISBN: 978-1-85345-374-8

2 Corinthians
Restoring harmony
ISBN: 978-1-85345-551-3

1 Timothy
Healthy churches –
effective Christians
ISBN: 978-1-85345-291-8

23rd Psalm
The Lord is my shepherd
ISBN: 978-1-85345-449-3

2 Timothy and Titus
Vital Christianity
ISBN: 978-1-85345-338-0

Acts 1-12
Church on the move
ISBN: 978-1-85345-574-2

Acts 13-28
To the ends of the earth
ISBN: 978-1-85345-592-6

Barnabas
Son of encouragement
ISBN: 978-1-85345-911-5

Bible Genres
Hearing what the Bible really says
ISBN: 978-1-85345-987-0

Daniel
Living boldly for God
ISBN: 978-1-85345-986-3

Ecclesiastes
Hard questions and
spiritual answers
ISBN: 978-1-85345-371-7

Elijah
A man and his God
ISBN: 978-1-85345-575-9

Ephesians
Claiming your inheritance
ISBN: 978-1-85345-229-1

Esther
For such a time as this
ISBN: 978-1-85345-511-7

Fruit of the Spirit
Growing more like Jesus
ISBN: 978-1-85345-375-5

Galatians
Freedom in Christ
ISBN: 978-1-85345-648-0

Genesis 1-11
Foundations of reality
ISBN: 978-1-85345-404-2

God's Rescue Plan
Finding God's fingerprints
on human history
ISBN: 978-1-85345-294-9

Great Prayers of the Bible
Applying them to our lives today
ISBN: 978-1-85345-253-6

Hebrews
Jesus – simply the best
ISBN: 978-1-85345-337-3

Hosea
The love that never fails
ISBN: 978-1-85345-290-1

Cover to Cover Every Day
Gain deeper knowledge of the Bible

Each issue of these bimonthly daily Bible-reading notes gives you insightful commentary on a book of the Old and New Testaments with reflections on a psalm each weekend by Philip Greenslade.

Enjoy contributions from two well-known authors every two months and over a five-year period you will be taken through the entire Bible.

Only £2.95 each (plus p&p)
£15.95 for UK annual subscription (bimonthly, p&p included)
£14.25 for annual email subscription
(available from www.cwr.org.uk/store)

 **Individual issues available in epub/Kindle formats**

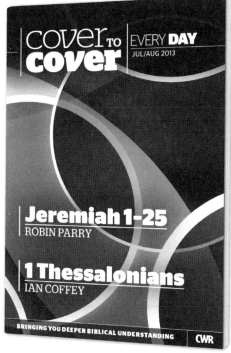

Prices correct at time of printing
To order visit www.cwr.org.uk/store
Available online or from Christian bookshops.

Cover to Cover Complete - NIV Edition
Read through the Bible chronologically

Take an exciting, year-long journey through the Bible, following events as they happened.

- See God's strategic plan of redemption unfold across the centuries
- Increase your confidence in the Bible as God's inspired message
- Come to know your heavenly Father in a deeper way

The full text of the NIV provides an exhilarating reading experience and is augmented by our beautiful:

- Illustrations
- Maps
- Charts
- Diagrams
- Timeline

And key Scripture verses and devotional thoughts make each day's reading more meaningful.

ISBN: 978-1-85345-804-0

For current price or to order visit www.cwr.org.uk/store
Available online or from Christian bookshops.